Original title:
Asteroid Belt Blues

Copyright © 2025 Creative Arts Management OÜ
All rights reserved.

Author: Aurora Sinclair
ISBN HARDBACK: 978-1-80567-857-1
ISBN PAPERBACK: 978-1-80567-978-3

## Orbiting Echoes

In the realm of rocks and dust,
A space dance we all trust.
Riding waves of cosmic cheese,
Dodging space junk with such ease.

With nibbles from a comet's tail,
Our laughter echoes in the pale.
We spin and glide, no time to snooze,
In this carefree cosmic cruise.

## **A Song for the Solitary**

A lone chunk drifts, all by itself,
No friends in sight, just space-shelf.
It croons a tune of meteor woes,
As it dreams of dances with space shows.

Wishing for a cosmic mate,
To share a laugh while they gravitate.
But alas, there's just deep silence,
It wobbles round, lacking guidance.

## Celestial Journeys

Round and round, like a merry-go,
Galactic winds whisper, 'Let's go!'
We'll surf the rings of Saturn's flair,
And share some jokes with the solar glare.

Navigating through the starry stew,
Each collision's a funny debut.
With a wink from Mars and a chuckle from Pluto,
It's a cosmic party, let's take it slow!

## **Nebula's Lament**

A cloud of color, but feeling blue,
Why does no one dance with you?
Gassy whispers float through space,
Seeking laughs, not just a trace.

Dreaming of a bright star's jest,
In the depths where the cosmos rest.
A comedy of errors in the night,
With swirling laughter, they take flight.

## The Silence of Space Rocks

In the void, rocks roll with glee,
Chasing each other, as wild as can be.
One says, "Hey, don't crash into me!"
They laugh and they twirl, oh what a spree!

Dust bunnies dance, a stellar ballet,
While comets just zoom, in a cosmic fray.
A meteor shouts, "I'm here for the play!"
But space is too quiet, what can they say?

## **Where Planets Weep**

Jupiter's storms, a swirling gray,
While Saturn just laughs, in rings of ballet.
Mars throws a tantrum, oh what a display,
Crying for water, far, far away.

Venus just giggles, all hot and bright,
While Mercury's sweating, with no end in sight.
Earth sends a wink, "You'll be alright,"
In the grand cosmic circus, a comical fright!

## Chasing Shadowed Trails

A rover rolls round, with tireless zeal,
Showing the universe all it can feel.
It waves to the stars, and spins with a wheel,
Shadows of laughter, in a cosmic reel.

Passing by Venus, it sings a groove,
"Hey planet, let's dance, come on, let's move!"
But Venus just pouts, in clouds it will prove,
While comets just giggle, in their own little groove!

## The Music of Cosmic Wanderings

Space filched a tune from a distant star,
Two moons jiving, playing guitars from afar.
Pluto joins in, no matter how bizarre,
Sings low and soft, a cosmic memoir.

Shooting stars twinkle, tapping their feet,
As black holes swirl, with a rhythm so sweet.
Galaxies mash up, a dancefloor complete,
In this cosmic party, none can beat!

## Sojourn Among the Stars

In a ship made of cheese and sweet cream,
We drift past a cosmic ice cream dream.
Planets juggle in their silvery gowns,
While comets toss confetti around in bounds.

My buddy's a toaster, he spreads on the jam,
Quoting old sci-fi like a quirky fam.
We giggle at meteors crashing on by,
And laugh as they fizzle, oh me, oh my!

Lost in the vastness, we play cards with stars,
Trading our thoughts for some moonbeams and bars.
A twinkle of laughter fills up the void,
As we ride through the cosmos, completely overjoyed.

So come, take a seat, let's share in this cheer,
Space travel's a hoot when you've got friends near.
We'll dance with the planets, with comets entwined,
In this cosmic circus, joyfully aligned.

## Spiraling into the Unknown

Zooming through space in our worn-out old pod,
With snacks made of stardust, we're getting quite flawed.
Gravity's on holiday, laughing with glee,
As we tumble and spin like a wild jubilee.

We met a green alien named Betty Lou,
Who baked us some cookies that tasted like glue.
Her pet was a three-legged creature named Fred,
Who plays tag in the vacuum, it's all in the head!

We're lost in the whirl of the Milky Way's dance,
Tripping on moon rocks, it's pure happenstance.
Oh, where are we headed? Who knows and who cares,
As we blast through the cosmos without any cares!

With laughter for fuel and smiles for our sails,
We'll navigate life through the moonlight trails.
So here's to the journey, the fun, and the wiles,
As we spiral through space, let's share all our smiles!

## Celestial Wanderers

In a realm where rocks do dance,
Planets chuckle, take a chance.
Comets race with goofy grins,
As they spin, just like old twins.

Asteroids roll in a jolly line,
Bumping into space, feeling fine.
With every twirl, a funny sight,
Cosmic clowns in the endless night.

They trade jokes in the cosmic breeze,
Bouncing off the moons with ease.
Shooting stars wink, share a laugh,
As they glide on their silly path.

Galaxies swirl, a vibrant crew,
In their orbits, they twist and skew.
With each misstep, just a cheer,
The universe chuckles, loud and clear.

## Echoes in the Cosmos

Out in space, where silence rules,
Whispers travel, playful schools.
Planets giggle, asteroids tease,
Singing songs carried with ease.

Cosmic echoes, a funny tune,
Bounce from Mercury to the moon.
In the void, they take their flight,
Stardust sparks in the cool night.

Silly meteors fly with glee,
Tickling asteroids, wild and free.
Their laughter rings, a soft parade,
Celestial pranks in a vast charade.

Every twinkle tells a joke,
In the dark, the stars provoke.
With a wink and a cosmic nod,
They share laughter, like an odd squad.

## Tumbling Through the Abyss

In the darkness, rocks collide,
Spinning tales they can't abide.
Gravity's pull is a funny foe,
As they tumble, in a row.

Each little chunk, a tale to spin,
Dodging stars, they grin and grin.
Floating past with goofy flair,
Meteors dance like they just don't care.

A rogue asteroid slips and slips,
Heading straight for cosmic trips.
With every swerve, it starts to laugh,
Claiming space like a silly giraffe.

Forgotten dreams through the deep sea,
Whispers of humor set them free.
In the vastness, they find their way,
Comedy rules in galactic play.

## **Dusty Dreams Among the Stars**

Among the stars, the dust does swirl,
A cosmic party, a whirling twirl.
Space debris in a frantic race,
Chasing giggles, leaving a trace.

Comets throw a glittery bash,
With fiery tails, they zoom and smash.
In their wake, they spill some jokes,
As they dance, the stardust pokes.

Distant planets share their puns,
Jovial laughter from celestial tons.
Each spin and flip, a sparkling glance,
In the void, they twist and prance.

Dreams of dust drift and glide,
Chasing laughter through the divide.
In the expanse, they make their mark,
Tales of whimsy in the dark.

## Dissonance of the Heavens

In the cosmos, rocks collide,
Singing songs we can't abide.
A melody of space debris,
With a catchiest of cacophony.

One rock winks, the other sighs,
Dodging dreams beneath the skies.
They giggle as they roll and spin,
In this dance where none can win.

Stars are laughing from afar,
At dust balls vying for a star.
A space brawl with no referee,
Where gravity's just a comedy.

So we launch our wishes wide,
While rocks jive in cosmic pride.
Round and round, what a sight!
Dissonance in the starlit night.

## Fragments of a Forgotten Galaxy

Once upon a time in flight,
Chunks of rock got quite a fright.
Lost in jokes from way back when,
Echoes of a quirky den.

The pebbles chat and strut around,
Spinning tales of silly sound.
In a whirl of cosmic cheer,
Who knew space could be so dear?

Old comets wave, as if to say,
"Hey there, let's joke and play!"
Each fragment's a punchline, you see,
Stuck in orbit, wild and free.

So here we are, dodging in lanes,
Riding laughter of old chains.
Galactic giggles all around,
In fragments, joy is always found.

## Between the Stars and Silence

In quiet space, the rocks are loud,
Whispering secrets, feeling proud.
A chuckle drifts through the void,
Of cosmic jokes that can't be avoided.

Between the stars, a jester glows,
With puns only a meteor knows.
Starlight twinkles, winks in delight,
At the foolishness of the night.

As silence gathers like a shroud,
The universe laughs—how very loud!
Cracks and pops of stardust jokes,
In between the cosmic folks.

So hold your breath, feel the tease,
Of space's funny little breeze.
In the quiet, humor roams,
Past the stars, we all find homes.

## Caught in the Cosmic Fray

Whirling, twirling, rocks collide,
In a chaos not disguised.
Bumping heads and giggling too,
Oh, what a sight in the cosmic view!

A runaway rock makes a splash,
In the dark, a wild dash.
They tell tall tales and play tag,
In a galaxy that's gone a bit ragged.

Each lump and bump has stories grand,
Sharing laughs in this vast land.
Caught in the fray like timid clowns,
Orbiting joy while spinning 'round.

So here we dance with dust and light,
In cosmic antics, pure delight.
Caught up in laughter, no dismay,
In the fray, we'll always play.

## **Celestial Sorrow**

In the sky where rocks collide,
I lost my snack, oh what a ride!
Floating crumbs like little stars,
Cheering me from cosmic bars.

Gravity waves messed with my chips,
Bouncing snacks, oh what a trip!
Asteroids laugh, they think it's grand,
While I'm dodging lunch in space's band.

## **Whispers of the Void**

In the quiet of endless black,
I hear whispers, a cosmic snack!
Meteors tease with tales of jam,
While I'm lost in an empty slam.

Rockets zoom past my confused brain,
Chasing burgers on a comet's train!
The universe smiles, it's all in jest,
While I'm stuck on this space food quest.

## Cosmic Road Trip

Pack your bags, we're off to roam,
Past Jupiter's clouds, we'll call it home!
With stellar tunes and ice cream moons,
We'll laugh at jokes from Martian cartoons.

Stop for gas at Saturn's rings,
Grab a snack, oh the joy it brings!
Aliens wave with soda in hand,
As we cruise through this empty land.

## Dance of Debris

Look at them spin, the rocks in flight,
Twisting and twirling in cosmic night!
Like disco balls in a stellar show,
While I just watch them spin and glow.

They groove past me, a wild parade,
While I'm lost in a space charade!
"No touching!" says the meteor crew,
As I attempt my own dance too.

## Nova of Nostalgia

In the cosmic dance, we twirl and spin,
Lost socks and old dreams all tumble in.
Galaxies giggle at our silly plight,
As we search for our snacks in the starlit night.

Cosmic crumbs stick to our starry shoes,
With each silly bounce, we laugh and snooze.
A nebula's grin, a supernova's cheer,
In this vast expanse, there's nothing to fear.

Floating past planets with names like Bob,
Who knew that space could feel like a blob?
We wave at a comet dressed up as a chef,
"Whatcha cooking, buddy?" we call with a clef.

Back to the start, we whistle and sing,
To the sounds of the cosmos, our voices take wing.
We dance with the meteors, all rotten and scuffed,
In this dance of the ages, we've all had enough!

## Celestial Dissonance

Oh, the planets argue, it's quite a sight,
Venus says, "I'm warmer, get it right!"
While Mars just grumbles, in a reddish fuss,
"Who needs you, I'm fine, just me and my dust!"

Jupiter laughs with its many moons,
Spinning round and round, playing silly tunes.
Uranus just giggles, a quirky old star,
In the cosmic karaoke, it sings from afar.

When the asteroids jive, it's a grand old time,
Bumping and bouncing, it's all in the rhyme.
"Who's got the rhythm?" one rock asks the next,
They tap dance along and feel quite perplexed.

And amidst all the noise, a comet drops by,
Waving hello with a twinkle in its eye.
"Hey, want to join my space circus today?"
Laughter erupts, and we all dance away!

## Voyage of the Lost Comets

Once upon a time, in a dusty old sky,
Comets got lost, oh my, oh my!
With trails like spaghetti, they wiggle and weave,
"Might we find ourselves? Let's not be naive!"

Through asteroid apples and planetary pies,
They traveled with giggles, not caring for size.
"Where's the cheese moon?" one comet cried out,
"Or the chocolate sun? Let's not miss our route!"

They huddled together, with thoughts of a feast,\nWhispering dreams of galactic yeast.
"Who brought the sprinkles?" a tiny one moaned,
As they zigzagged their way, clearly postponed.

But laughter was plenty, with stories to share,
Of dancing with stardust floating in air.
With a final hooray, they found their delight,
In the heart of a neutron, they settled in tight!

## The Weight of Floating Silence

In the void of the night, not a sound did we hear,
Just the weight of silence, floating near.
Stars held their breath, as we pondered the void,
"Where's the fun in space? I'm feeling destroyed!"

Through the black velvet, with a wink and a grin,
We summoned the giggles from deep within.
"Hey, black hole buddy, any jokes to share?"
"Just a few," it grumbled, "right after my lair."

And in this still place, thoughts tumbled around,
With thoughts of lost socks, and nonsense profound.
To planets unseen, we sent our bright cheer,
"If only the cosmos could lend us an ear!"

But the silence just chuckled, a tickle in space,
As we floated and pondered this age-old race.
In the weight of that quiet, we found a sweet tune,
"Let's dance with the meteors under the moon!"

### Echoes from the Edge

Floating rocks play peekaboo,
Nudging each other without a clue,
Cosmic chatter, oh what a mess,
Say hi to Kim, she's got a dress!

Tiny ships zoom in and out,
Space squirrels are what they tout,
Bumping along in zero G,
With a dance that's quite silly!

## **Starry Night Reverie**

Wish upon a twinkling star,
But don't aim for that dusty car,
Giggles echo from every nook,
As satellites share their own cookbook!

Meteor showers bring a grand show,
But don't get hit, just take it slow,
Jupiter's serving comet pie,
With a slice that makes you sigh!

### **Celestial Blues**

Space cows moo from asteroids bright,
Claiming it's an endless night,
Shooting stars play hopscotch round,
While space dust dances to the sound!

A vacuum cleaner sings a tune,
While stars giggle with the moon,
Cosmic cats in zero gravity,
Swaying along oh-so-funnily!

## **Between Orbit and Oblivion**

Planets chat while sipping tea,
Falling rocks think they're so free,
Comets crack jokes, oh what a show,
As planets whirl and twirl below!

Asteroids argue who's the best,
With silly hats, they jest and jest,
Galactic fun, a cosmic game,
In this great void, all's the same!

## The Color of Distant Worlds

Planets twirl in velvet nights,
With colors that give sight to fright.
One's a giant, party hat on,
The other grins like new dawn's spawn.

Floatin' rocks and icy peeps,
Dance around like sleepy sheep.
Each hue tells a silly tale,
Of cosmic strife and how they fail.

Timing's off, they miss their cues,
While splashing paint on coffee blues.
Galactic jokes just fly about,
As laughter echoes, full of doubt.

In a vast and goofy sprawl,
The orbit's just a fancy ball.
Distant worlds with winks and fun,
In this comedy, we all are one.

## An Odyssey Through Twilight

Blasting off in silly shades,
With snacks and drinks, we'll not trade blades.
Navigating through the afterglow,
With our tunes and cosmic flow.

Twilight giggles burst in space,
As comets join this merry chase.
Each twist and turn's a chance to grin,
Those cosmic bends, let the laughs begin.

The starry path's a trippy ride,
Full of jokes, our laughs collide.
Floating past a giant pie,
As Saturn waves, oh me, oh my!

In this odyssey, we find our groove,
The universe in silly moves.
Lost in fun, with beams and winks,
As twilight fades, the laughter links.

## Echoes of Lost Light

Light years start to play the fool,
While black holes whirl like a cosmic pool.
Stars that twinkle try their best,
To send out giggles from their nest.

Whispers dance in the void of space,
While shadows wear a grin and chase.
Echoes bounce with glee all night,
Making darkness seem so bright.

Lost light giggles through the haze,
While swirling orbits draw us mazes.
Every twinkle's like a jab,
In the silence, we just grab.

What fun we find in cosmic jest,
As echoes roll, we'll never rest.
The universe crackles with cheer,
In whispers that only we can hear.

## Cradled by the Cosmos

In the cradle of the night, we soar,
With stardust snacks galore to explore.
Galaxies hug us tight and warm,
Creating fun as we lose our norm.

Winking stars toss us bright cheer,
Like cosmic carousels we steer.
Floating rocks with giggly names,
Tickling space with silly games.

Gravity plays hide and seek,
While planets chirp, oh what a peek.
Each spark of light, a merry friend,
In this laughter that knows no end.

Cradled by the cosmic tease,
We spin and twirl with utmost ease.
The universe, a jester's tune,
As we whirl beneath the laughing moon.

## Celestial Conversations

In a twinkle, planets jest,
Stars engage in cosmic quests,
Comets laugh as they collide,
While black holes just try to hide.

Jupiter jokes, Saturn spins,
"Oh, those aliens," Mars grins,
Neptune shouts, 'I've got the best!'
While Pluto's feeling quite depressed.

## **Silence Among the Stars**

In the void, the silence cracks,
Aliens whisper in the snacks,
A meteor zips, makes a fuss,
While moons munch chips without a rush.

Galaxies gossip 'round the fire,
"Did you see that cosmic flyer?"
But all gets quiet when it's time,
For the solar wind's bedtime rhyme.

## Fractured Paths of Light

The photons trip on their own beams,
They chase their whispers, smash their dreams,
In a game of tag, the stars collide,
But everyone laughs, there's no need to hide.

Light-years stretch like silly strings,
While time dances with alien kings,
Gravity's not one to take a seat,
It's busy pulling at light's two left feet.

## The Weight of Starlight

Riding waves of shimmering light,
Stars wear capes and feel alright,
But who knew they had such weight?
Even starlight can be late!

They stack their beams like pancakes,
Dropping laughter, making mistakes,
Yet every twinkle brings delight,
As galaxies giggle 'til the night.

## Cosmic Whispers

In the dance of a cosmic ballet,
Tiny rocks spin and sway,
With laughter caught in their flight,
They play hide and seek in the night.

Floating on dreams of their own,
Each one claims a seat on the throne,
But they jostle and bicker for space,
Squeezing close in an odd little race.

With a wink and a mischievous grin,
They chuckle at the troubles within,
In the dark they share silly tales,
Of lost socks and balloons made ofails.

Oh, the giggles echo far and wide,
As they spin in an airy glide,
For even in their endless roam,
They find joy in a celestial home.

## The Lullaby of Dust

Whispering grains from days long gone,
They sing a tune as they bounce along,
Caught in the rhythm of a twinkling tide,
Dusty dreams in a galactic ride.

Floating between worlds like a lazy cat,
One moon giggles as it sees a bat,
A comet speed by giving a jest,
"Hey, watch me zoom, I'm the very best!"

While asteroids roll in a clumsy dare,
With tangled belts of feathery hair,
They toss silly jokes like shooting stars,
And paint the sky with their laughter's scars.

So, if you listen past the starry gleam,
You'll hear the cosmic dust's sweet dream,
In a chorus bright, they'll soothe the night,
With lullabies wrapped in starlit light.

## Twilight Among the Planets

In the twilight, the planets conspire,
To tell jokes and never tire,
With Saturn laughing, rings a-clatter,
As Mars quips, "Hey, does this matter?"

Neptune, blushing in deep shades of blue,
Says, "I once dated a star, it's true!"
Venus rolls eyes at the distant sun,
While Mercury zips, always on the run.

Asteroids giggle, a rosy-faced crew,
Trying to sneak in to hear what's new,
They tumble and tease with a cosmic flair,
In the shimmering space where no one cares.

So gather 'round, as the cosmos plays,
In their comedy act across the arrays,
They'll charm you with tales, both silly and grand,
In a show where the universe lends a hand.

## Gravity's Fragile Embrace

In the grip of a clumsy hold,
Gravity yanks, it's a sight to behold,
Stars stumble and trip in their cosmic spree,
While giggling at space's own comedy.

With a puff of dust and a fluttering song,
Tiny rocks wobble, where do they belong?
Asteroids flail, making merry mayhem,
"Can you keep up?" they shout, as they hem.

Floating together, a motley crew,
They share tales of what they've been through,
With snorts and chuckles, they wobble about,
Defying the pull, laughing without a doubt.

In this grand game of celestial tease,
They wiggle and jiggle with cosmical ease,
In the embrace of gravity's playful tug,
Life is a dance, with no need to shrug.

## Celestial Interludes

In a dance of dust and rocks,
The universe plays silly tricks.
Floating chunks in endless space,
Are they lost or just in a mix?

Who did this cosmic puzzle start?
One clumsy star with a messy heart.
It giggles as it spins around,
While we just watch, feeling quite smart.

Meteorites fling by like jokes,
A stellar laugh in hush of night.
Hey buddy, catch that one, oh wait!
Missed again—what a cosmic sight!

So let's toast to this space parade,
With floating snacks, in voids we wade.
Each chunk a friend in our grand quest,
To ponder what the stars have made!

## Fragments of a Cosmic Tapestry

Look at that rock, it looks like cheese,
A galactic snack, if you please!
Stars chuckle as they waltz about,
Throwing jokes in a cosmic breeze.

Zipping past with all their might,
Bumping into each other, what a sight!
Do they argue over all the space?
Or just laugh, spinning in delight?

A cratered ball sings a tune,
While comets swish like a large cartoon.
Each pebble knows its silly fate,
To drift and glide, and never swoon!

So let's gather these cosmic jesters,
In this grand galactic festival of testers.
With every twirl and wobble shared,
We find joy in the universe's jesters!

## **Vacuumed Melancholy**

In the emptiness, echoes do bleat,
A solitary rock sings bittersweet.
It wishes for a dance partner divine,
But finds only silence, a cosmic retreat.

Slipping through the vacuum's embrace,
Lonely chunks float in a space race.
A giggle here, a chuckle there,
In this void—it's quite the weird place!

What if they formed a band of their own?
Playing tunes on a comet's cyclone?
But the universe just rolls its eyes,
At the melancholic, stony tone.

Let's bring them joy with laughter's spark,
For even rocks want to leave their mark.
A swirling dance in this silent ball,
Enemies become friends in the dark!

## Shadows of the Great Beyond

Through the shadows, a rock does prance,
In the cosmic void, it takes a chance.
A little shimmy in the starlit gloom,
It's ready to risk a spacey romance!

Don't trip, oh chunk, on that solar flare,
Watch out for meteors, they don't care!
But here it twirls, with all its might,
In a universe that's more than fair.

Little buddies banter in the void,
With giggles and booms—oh, asteroid!
They dream of dancing in the sun's light,
Creating cosmic fun, never annoyed!

So let's cheer for these rocks that roam,
Their little jokes that light up the dome.
In the cosmic giggle, let's all take part,
For even stardust deserves a home!

## Lost in Gravity's Lullaby

In orbiting circles, I spin and twirl,
Chasing my snacks through the cosmic whirl.
A burger floats by, what a strange sight,
Starry-eyed dreams on a moonlit night.

With each little bump, I giggle and glide,
A dance with the comets, oh what a ride!
My space suit's a mess, but who even cares?
Lost in the laughter of stellar flares.

Asteroids chuckle, they wiggle and shake,
Playing a game, for goodness' sake!
I'm spinning 'round planets in wobbly glee,
Feeling like gravity's tickling me.

So here I float, in my cosmic clown,
Turning my frown upside down.
Giggles echo through the void so wide,
In this funny dream where I glide with pride.

## Celestial Serenade

Whispers of stardust, a melody sweet,
Floating on tunes that make me tap my feet.
Galactic gigs fill the vast night air,
Even black holes join in with flair.

Playful meteors light up the show,
Dancing and laughing, to and fro.
Singing in unison, a cosmic choir,
With each little quip, they spark a fire.

Funky space critters jump on a beam,
Slide through the rings, it's a wild dream.
Jovial echoes from planets so bright,
Have me twirling through the endless night.

Lost in the laughter, we waltz and play,
Making new rhythms, come join our ballet!
In this galaxy far, let giggles unfurl,
As I dance with the stars in a cosmic swirl.

## **Beyond the Brink of Stars**

Through zany trajectories, I wobble and spin,
Visit odd worlds, where chaos begins.
A place where sunbeams bounce off asteroids,
And laughter and mischief quite never avoids.

Giggling planets, with hats on their heads,
Popcorn comets dance 'round their beds.
Upside down moons lead a whirl of fun,
With sparkling laughter, rise with the sun.

Floating in circles, the joy never ends,
Among shooting stars, you'll meet your friends.
Galactic giggles echo through space,
What a wild, funny, and wondrous place!

Beyond the brink, where the quirks reside,
With each silly tumble, in joy we abide.
So grab your space shoes and join the throng,
In this cosmic carnival, where all belong.

## Cosmic Melancholy

In my little rocket, I ponder and muse,
Floating through cosmos with asteroid blues.
But wait! What's that? A bright comet's grin,
It tickles my heart, replaces the din.

Moody clouds frown, yet stars gleam anew,
In their shimmering jackets, with glittery hue.
Space squirrels chirp, 'Don't turn that frown!'
With nutty delights, they'll turn it around.

A galaxy filled with oddities rare,
Sings songs under starlight, without a care.
As I float by, I can't help but laugh,
At the cosmic joke, and my silly gaffe.

Though the orbits are strange and feelings can sway,
There's always a smile around the way.
In galactic jest, find joy in the gloom,
As laughter erupts through the cosmos' boom.

## **Nebula's Rhapsody**

In a space where rocks collide,
The laughter echoes wide.
Jokes are forged in cosmic dust,
As we float, we must adjust.

Meteors with silly grins,
Dance around like spinning twins.
Galactic pranks on every hand,
Is that a comet or a band?

Stars are winking far away,
They laugh at our clumsy play.
In this vast and funny scene,
We shake our heads at what we've seen.

So let's toast with stardust cheer,
To the laughs that echo here.
For life beyond the blue and green,
Is full of quirks yet unseen.

## Forlorn Pathways in the Sky

Through cosmic lanes, we stumble and sway,
Finding our way, but not today.
With asteroids on roller skates,
Who knew space could have such traits?

Elbowing through space's twist,
Dodging rocks we can't resist.
With each bump, we share a grin,
Floating high, we whiff the sin.

A satellite's got dance moves too,
How does it groove? I haven't a clue!
The void around us seems to chuckle,
In this stellar dance, we tumble and shuffle.

So onward we hop, with joy and jest,
In a galaxy where we're all guests.
Each pathway may seem forlorn,
But among friends, we're never torn.

## Drift and Dream in Endless Space

We drift among the starry schemers,
Spinning tales of cosmic dreamers.
The vacuums whisper silly jokes,
Like gravity's a clown in coats.

Black holes winking, pulling with glee,
"Come closer, let's eat your ship for tea!"
Space squids playing on infinite loops,
Counting stars in their goofiest groups.

Floating chairs in zero-gravity,
Who knew space held such depravity?
With giggles echoing through the night,
The universe sparkles, our shared delight.

So drift and dream, my cosmic friend,
In this vast stage, the fun won't end.
For every drift through the endless night,
Is a dance with silliness, sheer delight.

## **Rifts Among the Stars**

Rifts up high, where laughter flies,
Each comet's tail tells silly lies.
Jumping through the cosmic tears,
We shake with giggles and a few cheers.

Planets clash like cymbals loud,
A raucous band, a raucous crowd.
Dancing around ancient debris,
"Who's throwing rocks? It's not just me!"

Satellites can't keep their cool,
Twinkling like a jester's jewel.
In this wild galactic spree,
We're stardust fools, can't you see?

So let's embrace the cosmic jest,
In rifts where humor's truly blessed.
For among the stars, a playful muse,
Finds laughter where we dare to cruise.

**Blue Echoes from the Past**

In the silence of the night,
Old rocks spin with delight,
Telling tales of cosmic fun,
As they twinkle, a merry run.

Jupiter laughs, a big old clown,
While Saturn wears a ringed crown,
The stars chuckle, oh what a show,
Reminiscing as they glow.

Meteors make a clumsy dash,
In the dark, they take a splash,
Comets giggle as they streak,
While lost moons play hide and seek.

Fragments whisper silly jokes,
Past the orbits of old folks,
Galaxies shake their heads and sigh,
In this comedy up high.

## The Hearts of Fallen Giants

Once proud giants float away,
Their echoes dance where comets play,
Rocky hearts of olden lore,
Crash and tumble, need I say more?

Moon dust grins at all the fuss,
While asteroids form a vibrant bus,
They roll and bounce, a wobbly crew,
Stuck in space, they can't undo.

Galactic crumbs of broken dreams,
Whirl in laughter, or so it seems,
Finding joy in cosmic wrecks,
With sparkling smiles on those high specs.

Here in orbit, no cares to bear,
The giants giggle without a care,
For in their ruin lies delight,
An endless party in the night.

## Celestial Reverie

In a cosmic dance so grand,
Planets sway, take a stand,
Whispers from the void parade,
In this starlit escapade.

Wobbling rocks, a merry band,
In the sky, they twist and hand,
Chasing dreams on trails of light,
Tickling moons, oh what a sight.

Floating jesters, free and wild,
Laughing like a carefree child,
They scatter giggles, near and far,
In their realm, they're the stars.

So lift your gaze and share a smile,
Join the rocks and stay awhile,
In this reverie, joy is spun,
Where laughter, like stardust, runs.

**Dance of Cosmic Rocks**

Look at them twirl, these space-bound rocks,
Bouncing softly like playful socks,
They glide and slip without a care,
In the void, they twist and flare.

Comets join in, with tails so bright,
Dancing wildly, a silly sight,
Galactic tunes in every beat,
They form a chorus, oh so sweet.

Meteor showers rain with glee,
Twirling dust, oh can't you see?
Uranus chuckles, shakes its rings,
In this ballet, laughter sings.

As the universe spins and sways,
Join the fun in cosmic plays,
For in this dance of stellar jive,
The silly stones feel so alive.

## **Stardust Lament**

In the depths of space, I found my shoe,
Lost it near a comet, who knew?
It twirled in the void, a cosmic dance,
A match made with chaos, never a chance.

The stars winked at me, oh what a sight,
While asteroids laughed at my plight.
I shouted to Saturn, 'Send help, please!'
But all I got back was a mild solar breeze.

Through the void, my wallet did fly,
Tumbling past planets, oh me, oh my!
With space dust on fingers, I tried to pay,
But Martians don't take credit, I'm in dismay.

Now I'm sitting on Neptune, sipping cold brew,
With a view of the cosmos, a glorious hue.
I'll toast to my shoe, drifting away,
In this stellar circus, I'm here to stay.

## Orbiting Heartache

I wrote a love note and tossed it so high,
In hopes it would reach the blue sky.
But a satellite caught it, what a tease,
Now it's tangled in cables, salvaged with ease.

There was once a star, I had quite the crush,
But it blazed too bright and made me hush.
I waited for Venus, it never arrived,
Guess she's too busy, the cosmic vibe.

Sent my heart on a rocket to share,
But it went too fast, leaving me bare.
Now I just float with a grin, so wide,
Trying to capture love in the cosmic tide.

With rockets and laughter, I glide through the night,
In this sport of affection, I feel the delight.
Though orbits may shift and passions may wane,
I'll chase the starlight, through laughter and pain.

## Fragments of Forgotten Dreams

I found a dream on a meteor's tail,
It whispered, 'Chase me!', but I missed the trail.
With ice cream in hand, I took a wild ride,
Only to discover it had slipped inside.

The dust bunnies float as I ponder and sigh,
Why do my wishes just wave goodbye?
A tangle of wishes, like twinkling strands,
Play hide and seek in these cosmic lands.

My laughter echoes through the starry night,
As I juggle my dreams, oh what a sight!
With every misstep, I gamble and sway,
In this silly game where I always stray.

So let the comets chase my tripping feet,
In a galactic ballet, they just can't be beat.
With fragments of wishes, I'll dance all day,
In this crazy universe, come what may!

## Galactic Melancholy

In a nebula of giggles, I twisted my frown,
For space has its ways of turning me around.
I waltzed with a planet, so round and grand,
But tripped on a crater, oh wasn't that planned!

The moons had a party, I showed up too late,
They laughed as they orbited, such a fate!
With cake made of stardust, I tried to dive in,
But got stuck in a black hole, oh where have I been?

The cosmos can be such a tricky place,
With aliens chuckling at my slow pace.
Yet here in the vastness, I can't help but sing,
For every mishap's a new kind of bling.

So here's to the laughter, the bumps in the way,
In this galactic carnival, I'll dance and sway.
For melancholy might linger, just like a tune,
But I'll turn it around, dancing under the moon.

## **Dance of the Celestial Wanderers**

In a swirling dance, they twirl with glee,
Rocky little orbs, so wild and free.
With cookie crumbs and cosmic pies,
They laugh and spin beneath the skies.

One plucky chunk trips, oh what a sight!
Says, "Look at me, I'm taking flight!"
But bounces back, with a chuckle so grand,
That's the charm of this roaming band.

Stardust glitters in their play,
As they roll and bounce throughout the day.
"Catch me if you can!" one shouts with mirth,
Yet they float along, giving no dearth.

And if they collide, it's all in jest,
A cosmic giggle, they laugh at the quest.
With comet tails trailing their carefree spree,
These wanderers dance, wild and free!

## The Grief of Gravity

Oh, gravity, you keep us down,
While we dream of stars in a far-off town.
A rock dreams big, but alas, it's stuck,
"Where's my lift?" it cries, just out of luck.

A cosmic crowd, they wail and weep,
While nearby rocks just roll and creep.
"Not fair!" they shout, "I want to float!"
Yet all they do is bicker and gloat.

A comet zooms past, with a wink and a grin,
"Hey, cheer up! Just take a spin!"
But lumps of stone can only sigh,
As the starry ship sails ever high.

They cast their wishes on a silver beam,
Hoping one day to join the dream.
Till then, they'll grumble, giggle, and pout,
In this playful universe, laughing about.

## Songs of Starlit Solitude

In the silence of space, a lonely rock sings,
Humming by itself about wonderful things.
"Wish I had friends for a game of catch,
But here I am, no one to match."

Twinkling stars snicker from miles away,
"Oh, lonely lump, why not play?
We'll send you tunes from up high in the mist,
Just don't forget us, with your cosmic twist!"

A craggy smile forms, as tunes fill the void,
He taps to the rhythm, feeling overjoyed.
"Though friends are few, I've got my sound,
In this vast expanse, joy's still around."

So he dances alone, with a cosmic flair,
You might find him gliding without a care.
In the songs of solitude, laughter flows free,
As the universe hums its sweet symphony!

## Celestial Postcards

Floating through space, they send out a line,
With cosmic postcards to friends who shine.
"Wish you were here!" each message begins,
While tiny rocks laugh at their simple spins.

"Greetings from Mars, we're having a ball!"
One postcard reads, "Come, join us all!"
But the belts have no maps, and they're stuck where they roam,
Sending their postcards, feeling at home.

A postcard from Jupiter, with storms oh so wild,
Says, "Oh, bumpy space, you're still my child!"
But no one replies, as the letters drift on,
Just wandering bits until they are gone.

Yet in all this chaos, they chuckle and beam,
"Though we're far apart, we're still a great team!"
So they send off their cards with a comet's swift flare,
For the love of the cosmos glides everywhere!

## The Weight of Lightyears

The light is slow, it takes its time,
Stars grinning wide, oh what a climb.
A cosmic traffic jam, we can't complain,
Every lightyear lingers, it's part of the game.

Gravity's pulling, but hey, we float,
In this endless sea, we'll sail and gloat.
Jokes fly faster than the speed of light,
Who knew interstellar could feel so right?

With comets laugh, and moons that dance,
Floating on dreams, all caught in a trance.
Rockets with rubber bands, what a sight,
Who needs engines when laughter's the might?

So here's to the giggles, the cosmic chuckles,
In the endless sprawl where gigabytes snuggle.
We're all just stardust, laughing 'til dawn,
In this great wide expanse, boredom's long gone.

## Wandering Among Giants

Giant balls of gas, they just can't sit still,
Dancing in space, with their own kind of thrill.
They wobble and sway, oh what a sight,
Giving each other nudges, just out of spite.

With belts of rocks that sparkle and shine,
We whirl through the cosmos, feeling just fine.
Drawing doodles on Saturn's rings of ice,
Creating our graffiti, oh isn't that nice?

Jupiter laughs, with a storm in his eyes,
While Neptune just shivers, under starry skies.
Pluto's grumpy, he's lost in the fray,
"Can I come join?" we hear him say.

Among these giants, we twirl and spin,
Collecting the giggles where the stars begin.
So roll out the carpet, let's dance on the beams,
In our cosmic playground, we'll chase our dreams.

## Nomads of the Night Sky

We drift like balloons on a calm summer's night,
Searching for laughter, our hearts take flight.
With a wink from the moon, we plot and we scheme,
Riding on meteors, chasing our dream.

Galactic hitchhikers, with stars in our eyes,
Trading old tales, 'neath the shimmering skies.
A joke here, a lark there, we share with delight,
In this cosmic carnival, life feels so bright.

With every rotation, we find more fun,
Underneath constellations, we're never outdone.
Galaxy hopping, with giggles galore,
On this long space road, there's always much more.

So here's to the nomads, lost but not sad,
Celebrating the cosmos, the good and the bad.
With laughter as currency, we make our way,
Through the universe's wonders, come what may.

## Tales from the Fractured Orbit

Around and around in a fractured embrace,
Planets collide, oh what a race!
With each little bump, we chuckle and cheer,
Finding amusement in space's bright sphere.

A comet slips by with a wink and a grin,
Telling secrets of where he has been.
Saturn's rings jingle, like bells in the void,
Their harmony's silly, never destroyed.

We gather the stardust, we spin and we sway,
Creating wild stories at the close of the day.
Each twinkling light holds a tale to unfold,
In this colorful circus, both vivid and bold.

So here's to the orbits, all fractured and free,
Telling our stories for all to see.
In this zany universe, laughter's our play,
We'll dance through the chaos, come what may!

## Celestial Drift

Floating through space, what a sight,
Lost among rocks, day and night.
Dodging debris, it's quite a ride,
Gravity's pull, nowhere to hide.

Waving to comets, like old friends,
In this vast playground, the fun never ends.
With each little bump, I giggle a cheer,
Hoping a meteor won't come too near.

I sip stardust smoothies, oh what a treat,
While planets do ballet on their cosmic beat.
Dancing round Saturn, I give a grand twirl,
And chuckle at Earthlings, just a small world.

So here's to the drift, let's float and fray,
In the wacky expanse where we play all day.
For who needs a plan in this stellar domain?
Just me and my laughter, in the cosmic train.

**Orbiting Solitude**

In the shadows of giants, I make my own way,
Circling in silence, where planets sway.
With a wink to the stars, I feel so alive,
In this quirky ballet, I happily thrive.

A lonesome parade of space junk and bliss,
Echoes of laughter in a celestial hiss.
Asteroids twirl, like they learned in ballet,
Spinning their tales in a whimsical way.

Starship snacks, oh the galactic gust,
Nibbling on meteorites, it's simply a must.
With my cosmic companions, bright and bizarre,
Orbiting solitude feels like a star.

So here's to the orbit, my solo cheer,
Where even the silence sings loud and clear.
Each twist and each turn, I grin ear to ear,
In my silly little world, I've nothing to fear.

## Dusty Trails of the Cosmos

On dusty trails where stardust flies,
I skip through the cosmos, no need for ties.
With a wink to the moons, I prance and I leap,
Over craters and comets, in galactic sweep.

Waddling past nebulae with trails so bright,
I laugh with the shadows that dance in the night.
Each meteor that zips gives me quite a thrill,
Like a cosmic carnival, it's never still.

Space squirrels are gathering their galactic nuts,
While aliens giggle, in their shiny huts.
They wave and they holler, come play with us too,
In these dusty trails where the fun is anew.

So let's wander freely, no map to constrict,
Embracing the dust that makes life picturesque.
In the trails of the cosmos, with laughs that abound,
I find joy in the journey, where wonder is found.

## **Chasing Celestial Shadows**

Chasing shadows of planets, I race through the void,
With laughter and glee, I feel overjoyed.
Dancing with comets like stars in disguise,
In this cosmic frolic, I see through wise eyes.

Juggling stardust with a flourish and flair,
My interstellar show is quite rare, I swear!
Saturn's rings giggle, they shimmer and shine,
While I twirl through the space, feeling simply divine.

With my shadowy friends, we play hide and seek,
Between asteroid fragments, we hide every week.
A chuckle erupts when we bump and collide,
In this funny ballet, where joy can't subside.

So onward I chase, in this magical race,
With shadows as partners, I find my place.
Each giggle and twist, a whimsical dance,
In this wondrous realm, where we jump at the chance.

## Wanderlust Among the Stars

In a ship made of cheese, I glide through the night,
Dodging space rocks that glitter, oh what a sight.
A comet sneezes as I pass by fast,
With laughter I travel, I'm having a blast.

Planets are playing a cosmic game,
Saturn's rings whisper, 'What's in a name?'
Mars sends a postcard that's covered in dust,
In this interstellar, I wander with trust.

Galaxies twirl like a grand ballet,
Sunbeams are dancing, come join their play.
With stardust confetti, I throw up my hands,
Adventures in space, oh, aren't they grand?

A vacuum that swallows my jokes with a grin,
But I'll keep on telling, it's all in the spin.
Laughs echo through cosmos, that infinite sea,
In my space-bound delight, I'm forever carefree.

## Separation in Space

Floating apart like two lost balloon,
Whispers of stardust, a comical tune.
One moon spins left, the other turns right,
Who knew love could travel at light-speed in flight?

We wave from afar, with eyebrows that raise,
Comets do chuckle in this star-studded maze.
Your planet's so green, mine's just a rock,
Guess I'll send my hugs via space-time clock!

Late-night zoom chats through asteroid streams,
You tell me my jokes burst apart at the seams.
Yet laughing together, we giggle and grin,
What's distance in space when we're thick as the skin?

Planets may roll, but our humor won't fade,
Wrapped up in laughter, we weave our charade.
So here's to our journey, each twinkle and space,
Even apart, you'll forever hold a special place.

## **Cosmic Dissonance**

Stars clash and clang in a galactic band,
Dropping beats and rhythms that no one quite planned.
Black holes are crooning, with echoes that sway,
In this quirky concert, we dance and we play.

The asteroids jam like they own the whole night,
Bumping and grinding in chaotic delight.
I tried to play trumpet but twisted a tune,
Now I serenade aliens beneath the bright moon.

Saturn's rings shimmer like a disco ball,
While Mars grooves solo, 'ain't got no walls.'
The Milky Way thumps with a beat so divine,
A cosmic cacophony, and soon I'll be fine.

Yet between every note, I chuckle and grin,
For the sound of the cosmos is where we begin.
So bring on the discord, let laughter unite,
In this funny symphony of day turning night.

## Silent Chords of the Universe

Whispers of starlight dance in the void,
Hums of the cosmos, where silence is toyed.
I tune into galaxies with my ears open wide,
Strumming the chords of this spacious ride.

Nebulas blush like they're caught in a dare,
While comets prance past like they don't have a care.
Gravity's tugging, but who's keeping score?
In this tune of the silence, I'm ready for more.

A black hole hiccups, oh what a surprise,
Flinging jokes at meteors, see how they fly.
Each twinkling star winks with mirth in their glow,
A riddle of laughter where no one can go.

So here is my song, unhurried, unplanned,
A serenade drifting through this funny land.
With cosmic chords strummed on an ethereal wave,
In the silence of space, we learn how to rave.

www.ingramcontent.com/pod-product-compliance
Lightning Source LLC
Chambersburg PA
CBHW072138200426
43209CB00050B/116